W9-AVZ-311

Birthday Surprise

by Deborah Schecter

ISBN-13: 978-0-545-25757-2 / ISBN-10: 0-545-25757-3

Illustrated by Anne Kennedy
Designed by Maria Lilja • Colored by Ka-Yeon Kim-Li
Copyright © 2010 by Deborah Schecter

■SCHOLASTIC

I have paper.

I have glue.

I have stickers.

I have crayons.

I have a birthday card for you!

I have scissors.

I have ribbon.